HANDS-ON SCIENCE

FUN MACHINES

Step-by-Step Science Activity Projects
from the Smithsonian Institution

Gareth Stevens Publishing
MILWAUKEE

For a free color catalog describing Gareth Stevens' list of high-quality books, call 1-800-542-2595 (USA) or 1-800-461-9120 (Canada). Gareth Stevens' Fax: (414) 225-0377.

Library of Congress Cataloging-in-Publication Data

Hands-on science. Fun machines / by Megan Stine . . . [et al.] ; illustrated
   by Simms Taback.
            p.   cm. -- (Hands-on science, step-by-step science activity projects from
      the Smithsonian Institution)
      Series originally published by the Smithsonian Institution as a series of science
activity calendars.
      Includes bibliographical references and index.
      Summary: Provides instructions for making such devices as a tin-can
telegraph, crystal radio, and kaleidoscope, and suggests a variety of related
experiments and other activities.
      ISBN 0-8368-0956-4
      1. Science--Experiments--Juvenile literature. 2. Scientific recreations-
-Juvenile literature. 3. Machinery--Design and construction--Juvenile
literature. [1. Science--Experiments. 2. Scientific recreations. 3. Experiments.
4. Machinery--Design and construction.] I. Stine, Megan. II. Taback, Simms, ill.
III. Series: Hands-on science (Milwaukee, Wis.).
Q164.H246   1993
680'.78--dc20   92-56891

Produced and published by
Gareth Stevens Publishing
1555 North RiverCenter Drive, Suite 201
Milwaukee, Wisconsin 53212, USA

This edition © 1993 by the Smithsonian Institution. First published by
the Smithsonian Institution and Galison Books, a division of GMG Publishing,
as a series of Science Activity Calendars.

Series editor: Patricia Lantier-Sampon
Book designer: Sabine Beaupré
Editorial assistants: Jamie Daniel and Diane Laska

Printed in the United States of America

2 3 4 5 6 7 8 9 9 99 98 97 96 95 94

CONTENTS

Weights and Measures Abbreviation Key

U.S. Units

in = inch	oz = ounce	
ft = foot	qt = quart	
tsp = teaspoon	gal = gallon	
T = tablespoon	lb = pound	
C = cup	°F = °Fahrenheit	

Metric Units

cm = centimeter	kg = kilogram
m = meter	km = kilometer
ml = milliliter	°C = °Centigrade
l = liter	
g = gram	

INTRODUCTION

By the 21st century, our society will demand that all its citizens possess basic competencies in the fundamentals of science and technology. As science becomes the dominant subject of the workplace, it is important to equip children with an understanding and appreciation of science early in their lives.

Learning can, and does, occur in many places and many situations. Learning occurs in school, at home, and on the trip between home and school. This book provides suggestions for interactive science activities that can be done in a variety of settings, using inexpensive and readily available materials. The experiments, activities, crafts, and games included in this book allow you, whether teacher or parent, to learn science along with the children.

SOME SUGGESTIONS FOR TEACHERS

The activities in this book should be used as supplements to your normal classroom science curricula. Since they were originally developed for use in out-of-school situations, they may require some minor modifications to permit a larger number of children to participate. Nonetheless, you will find that these activities lend themselves to a fun-filled science lesson for all participants.

SOME SUGGESTIONS FOR PARENTS

One of the most important jobs you have as a parent is the education of your children. Every day is filled with opportunities for you to actively participate in your child's learning. Through the **Hands-On Science** projects, you can explore the natural world together and make connections between classroom lessons and real-life situations.

FOR BOTH TEACHERS AND PARENTS

The best things you can bring to each activity are your experience, your interest, and, most importantly, your enthusiasm. These materials were designed to be both educational and enjoyable. They offer opportunities for discovery, creative thinking, and fun.

HOW TO USE THIS BOOK

There are ten activities in this book. Since every classroom and family is different, not all activities will be equally suitable. Browse through the book and find the ones that seem to make sense for your class or family. There is no prescribed order to these activities, nor any necessity to do all of them.

At the beginning of each activity is a list of all the materials you will need to do the project. Try to assemble all of these items before you begin. The procedures have been laid out in an easy-to-follow, step-by-step guide. If you follow these directions, you should have no difficulty doing the activity. Once you have completed the basic activity, there are also suggested variations that you can try, now or later. At the end of each activity is an "Afterwords" section to provide additional information.

TIN-CAN TELEGRAPH

TIN-CAN TELEGRAPH

The telegraph was invented in 1837 by Samuel F.B. Morse. This simple gadget first made it possible to receive messages within an instant after they were sent! Take about 30 minutes to build your own telegraph and discover how messages can be relayed by electricity.

YOU WILL NEED

1 #303 Tin can (such as a
    1-pound vegetable can)
Can opener
1 10-Foot length of #20
    insulated wire
1¼" Steel bolt about 3" long
Pliers
Scissors
1 "D" battery
Sandpaper, fine or
    medium grade
Masking tape

A telegraph operates on *electromagnetism*. A tiny magnetic field is formed around a wire when electricity flows through it. By wrapping the wire around a steel bolt, the bolt will become magnetic, too — once the electrical circuit has been completed, or *closed*. You can arrange it so that each time the circuit is closed, the magnet attracts a piece of steel and they come together with a loud *click!* And that's what makes a telegraph!

1 Use a can opener to cut the top of the tin can completely off. *Save the top!* Clean the can and remove the label. Cut the bottom *most* of the way off, but not completely: Leave a ¾" section uncut.

2 Use pliers to bend the edges of the still-connected lid, as shown: first the two edges, then the tip. This is your flapper. Then squeeze the can (fingers should be under the flapper and on the side opposite where it is still attached to the can) until the can becomes an oval shape. Bend the flapper down so that it sticks out over the edge of the can.

3 Cut 6" of wire from the 10-foot length. Strip about 1" of the insulation from both ends of the long *and* short pieces of wire. (To do this, use scissors to cut through the plastic insulation, applying a *very gentle* pressure so that you won't cut all the way through to the wire.) Wrap the long wire around the bolt *very neatly,* placing one loop right next to the last one wrapped. Make sure you leave about 6" of each end of the wire sticking out. Wrap some tape around the wound-up wire to keep it in place.

4 Securely tape one end of this long wire to one end of the "D" battery and one end of the short wire

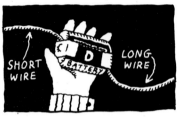

to the other end of the battery. Be sure to put plenty of tape on both ends of the battery.

5 Now take the other lid that you removed and saved, and use the pliers to bend back the sharp edges, just as you did for the flapper. *However,* before you do the last edge, pinch the other end of the *short* wire into the fold. **But first:** Use sandpaper to rub away any coating on the can lid, at the spot where the wire will make contact. Now you've made your "telegraph key."

6 Now assemble the telegraph. Tape the bolt to the side of the can so the head of the bolt is right under the tip of the flapper, about ⅛″ away. Wrap the tape around the bolt and can several times. Wedge the battery into the bottom of the can.

7 Tape the key to the side of the can as illustrated. Tape the remaining exposed end of the long wire to the can *under* the free end of the key, but *not* touching it. Now, when you press down on the key, it contacts the bare wire, the circuit is completed, the magnetized bolt pulls down the flapper, and the Tin-Can Telegraph

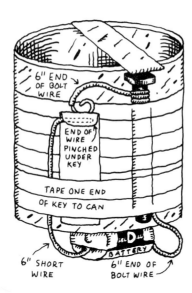

6″ END OF BOLT WIRE

END OF WIRE PINCHED UNDER KEY

TAPE ONE END OF KEY TO CAN

BATTERY

6″ SHORT WIRE

6″ END OF BOLT WIRE

goes *click, click, click!* **Note:** If the flapper sticks to the bolt, increase the distance between the end of the flapper and the head of the bolt. If the flapper

won't pull over to the bolt, check your circuit, adjust the gap, or get a new battery.

8 Make up a simple code comprised of clicks (1 click = A, 2 clicks = C, 3 clicks = E, 4 clicks = R, etc.) and take turns using the telegraph to send messages. So, to send the word "race," the sender would key 4 clicks, followed by 1 click, then 2 clicks, and finally 3 clicks.

Actually, old Sam Morse not only popularized the telegraph, he also developed a code for sending messages. The individual clicks sent by the telegraph were separated from one another by either a short interval or a long inter-

SIMPLE CODE
1 CLICK = A
2 CLICKS = C
3 CLICKS = E
4 CLICKS = R

val. It was actually the pattern of long and short pauses between clicks that early Morse code users listened to. Today we refer to the code as being made up of *dots* and *dashes*. You can find the Morse code in an encyclopedia or dictionary and use it to send some messages. The easiest way to practice is to use a fingernail on a piece of wood, tapping for the "dots" and scratching for the "dashes."

CLICK CLICK CLICK CLICK
CLICK
CLICK CLICK CLICK
CLICK CLICK

AFTERWORDS

If you saw some friends waiting down the street, what would you do to get their attention? You would probably yell, maybe whistle, even wave your arms in the air. But what if they were several blocks away? They probably wouldn't be able to hear your shouts or see your arm signals. This is the problem of *telecommunication* (*tele* means "distant"). So how can we communicate at a distance?

One of the earliest forms of telecommunication was pounding on a hollow log with a stick. The next step was to stretch and dry animal skins over the ends of these hollow logs to form drums. A pattern of beats was established to warn of approaching danger or to call people together. But still you had to be close enough to hear the drums to get the message.

Visual signals developed around the same time as sound signals. For example, early American Indians used smoke signals. Messages were also sent by lighting fires on hilltops or beaches. Paul Revere used lighted lanterns to warn of danger during the American Revolution. (Remember "one, if by land; two, if by sea"?) The U.S. Navy still communicates from ship to ship by flashing lights — especially if they don't want to use their radios for fear that the enemy might tune in. The Navy also sends messages between ships with *semaphore* flags: A flag is held in each hand and the different flag positions indicate different letters of the alphabet. Colored lights along railways, near airports, on high buildings and floating buoys, and at traffic intersections are all visual signals that communicate simple messages to us.

But all these light and sound systems of telecommunication are limited by how far you can see or hear. Luckily, once electricity was discovered it wasn't long before electronic ways of telecommunicating were developed. The telegraph, invented by Samuel Morse, was the first practical electronic communicator. Morse was not a skilled scientist, but his curiosity and imagination helped him organize the work of others into a useful machine. In 1843, Congress gave Morse money to run a telegraph line from Washington to Baltimore. Messages "clicked" out with a metal key that could be heard on the receiving end or be printed out onto paper tape. The first telegraphed message was sent on May 24, 1844.

Finally, Alexander Graham Bell developed the telephone in 1876. Both the telegraph and the telephone use electromagnets that need a wire between sender and receiver. But once radio waves (an electromagnetic wave with a radio frequency) were discovered, radio transmitters and receivers were created to send messages through the air *without* wires. Long and complex messages can now be sent all over the world at the speed of light — 186,000 miles in 1 second!

Today's modern message magic uses satellites that stay in a fixed position in space. Electromagnetic waves from televised events such as the Olympic Games in Yugoslavia bounce off these satellites' and turn up on televisions in American living rooms. We've certainly come a long way from pounding a hollow log!

1/8 in = .32 cm	1 1/4 in = 3.2 cm
3/4 in = 1.9 cm	3 in = 7.6 cm
1 in = 2.54 cm	6 in = 15.2 cm
10 ft = 3.1 m	1 lb = .45 kg
186,000 mi = 299,274 km	

SOUND MACHINE

SOUND MACHINE

3/4 in x 10 in x 16 in =	
1.9 cm x 25 cm x 41 cm	8 in = 20.3 cm
1/2 in = 1.27 cm	10 in = 25.4 cm
12 oz = 340 g	12 in = 30.5 cm
1 in = 2.54 cm	18 in = 45.7 cm
6 in = 15.2 cm	14 in = 35.6 cm

The hour that it takes to make your stringed instrument will provide many hours of fun for you and friends as you experiment with sound.

YOU WILL NEED

1 Piece of smooth wood (used for shelves) ¾" ×10" ×16"
10 Short (1") nails
2 Yards of clear nylon string or fishing line (strong enough to support about 20 pounds; this is available in most hardware stores)
1 1" wooden block
Hammer, scissors, pencil
Ruler, empty 12-ounce soda bottle

Have you ever been hit by a sound wave? If so, you probably didn't mind it. No, this is not one of those corny jokes like seeing a cigar box or butter fly. A sound wave is a kind of movement that travels through the air or other substance and is picked up by our ears as sound. These movements can be small waves that move very fast and come very close together. They can move slowly and be far apart. You will be able to hear the difference between them by building a stringed instrument. Then just pluck the strings and let the sound waves hit your ears.

1 On your piece of wood, make 5 pencil marks in a straight line, beginning about 1 inch down from the 10 inch side, and about 1 inch apart. Cut the nylon string into 5 pieces of the following lengths: 14 inches, 12 inches, 10 inches, 8 inches, 6 inches.

2 Make a slip knot on each end of each piece of nylon and, leaving the knots loose, put a nail into one loose slip knot on the

SLIP KNOT

longest piece of string and pull it as tight as you can. Then at the first pencil mark at either edge of the wood, hammer the nail into the wood (about ½ inch). One half of the nail will be showing.

3 Put a nail into the loose slip knot on the other end of the thread and pull it as tight as you can. Then pull the string straight and very tight. Hammer the nail into the wood at that point (about ½ inch deep).

4 Repeat Steps 1 through 4 with each piece of nylon. Use a shorter piece each time, until you have used the shortest available string, which is 6".

HOW TO MAKE DIFFERENT SOUND WAVES

When each string is tightly in place, your instrument is ready to play! Pluck each string separately with your second or third finger. Does each one make a different sound? Which string makes the lowest sound or has the lowest pitch? Which one makes the highest sound or has the highest pitch? You will notice that the longer the string, the lower the sound or pitch. The shorter the string, the higher the pitch. The longer strings vibrate, or move back and forth, more slowly than the shorter ones. The waves or air movements made by the longer strings are wider or farther apart. The waves or air movements made by

the shorter strings are faster and closer together.

■ Put the little 1-inch block of wood underneath the middle of the longest string. Pluck the string on both sides of the block. Has the pitch changed?

Move the block along underneath the string. See what happens when you pluck the string on both sides after each move. Move the block back and forth and play a tune. You probably can if

you use all the strings. Each time you put the little block of wood under a string, you make two shorter strings, and the sound waves for each one move more quickly. The pitch you hear is higher each time.

VARIATIONS

■ Hold a 12-inch or 18-inch ruler firmly on the edge of a desk so that about 10 inches of the ruler sticks out over the edge of the desk. Now pull the free end down gently and

THE SOUND ~~NEW~~ WAVE MUSIC ORCHESTRA

11

let it go. Repeat the pull, but do it harder. The more energy you use, the greater air disturbance or more sound waves there are. The more energy, the louder the sound. Now try pulling the ruler down with less of the ruler sticking out over the edge of the desk. Does the sound change? Is it higher or lower? You can probably understand why it is higher.

■ Get an empty soda bottle (12-ounce, without a cap). Hold the bottle up to your mouth. Press your lower lip gently against the neck of the bottle and blow sharply across the open top of the bottle. Do this several times until you are able to make a good "toot" each time. Then put about 1 inch of water in the bottle and blow again. Has the sound changed? Add a little more water and blow again. Each time, the sound is higher.

■ Ask 4 or 5 friends each to get an empty bottle and join you. One bottle should stay empty. Put a different amount of water in each of the other bottles. Now get your Bottle Band together and play some tunes. Just by changing the amount of water in each bottle, you can change the pitch of each bottle, and blow a different note.

AFTERWORDS

Have you ever seen an eardrum? Probably not, but each time you plucked a string on your stringed instrument or blew across the top of a soda bottle, you disturbed the air and made waves that finally hit your eardrum. Your eardrum then began to vibrate or to move back and forth.

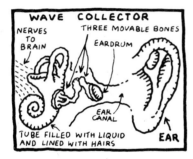

When an object, say a pin or a rhinoceros, moves, it bumps into the small particles or molecules that surround it. These molecules may be air, liquid, or solid. Before these moving molecules can bounce back, they bounce into other molecules, which then bounce into more molecules. While each molecule only moves slightly, the sound of a pin dropping or a rhino snorting may travel a long distance over a road of moving molecules. Finally, the molecules reach your ear. They bump into your eardrum, which begins to vibrate. Your nerve endings carry these vibrations to your brain and your brain translates them into sound.

Sound waves are a series of movements in molecules. If you could see sound waves, they would look like the rings of ripples made when a stone is dropped into water. Sound ripples spread from the source of movement or vibration — the dropping pin, the snorting rhino. When molecules bump together, they cause compressions; when they move apart, they cause expansions. You can picture this when you pluck your stringed instrument. As the nylon string is stretched up, it moves the air molecules above it (compression) and thins out those below it (expansion). As the string snaps downward, it does the opposite: It compresses the air molecules below and those above it expand. As they expand, they compress the molecules beyond them. As long as the string vibrates, you can hear the air disturbance as a "twang."

If we could see sound waves, they would look like ocean waves. The top or crest of the wave would show compression. The bottom or trough between would show expansion. The taller the wave, the louder the sound. The faster the waves, the higher the pitch or frequency. Your ear is shaped like a funnel to collect sound waves. It funnels the waves to your eardrum. The waves set the eardrum in motion and it pushes against three small bones. The last bone is attached to a coiled tube filled with liquid. As the eardrum moves, it sets the bones moving. The last bone sets the liquid in motion. The liquid pushes against tiny hairs that line the tube or ear canal. These hairs are connected to the nerves that transmit the rhythm, speed, and strength of the movement to the brain. Then we say that we "hear."

How the brain translates this movement into what we hear is not yet understood. It may be that what we know as sound is something we invent inside our heads.

CRYSTAL RADIO

CRYSTAL RADIO

5.5 in x 8.5 in = 13.9 cm x 22 cm	17 in = 43.2 cm
8.5 in x 11 in = 22 cm x 27.9 cm	18 in = 45.7 cm
1/8 in = .32 cm 7 in = 17.8 cm	1 ft = .3 m
1 in = 2.54 cm 8 in = 20.3 cm	20 ft = 6.1 m
4 in = 10.2 cm 10 in = 25.4 cm	30 ft = 9.1 m
6 in = 15.2 cm 12 in = 30.5 cm	50 ft = 15.2 m

Tune in to what's happening —on your own homemade crystal radio. No batteries required! The radio can be made in about an hour and a half. And it can be listened to *forever*—or at least until bedtime.

YOU WILL NEED

1 Empty plastic film canister (the kind a roll of 35mm film comes in)
Scissors
1 Piece of corrugated cardboard, 7" by 18"
Heavy-duty aluminum foil
Transparent tape
Masking tape
2 Sheets of 8½" by 11" paper
2 Spring-type clothespins, or 2 large, spring-action paper clips

From an electronics store, such as Radio Shack:
50 Feet of 22-gauge solid, insulated hook-up wire
1 Germanium diode
1 Phono input cable with plug (one end of the cable should already be stripped)

Note: You will also need access to a stereo amplifier and speakers, in order to hear the signal from your crystal radio.

What's a crystal radio? It's a radio made out of some wire, cardboard, aluminum foil, and very little else. The only mysterious thing in a crystal radio is the germanium crystal diode—and it's not really so mysterious. Germanium is a metal that can help detect radio waves. In fact, under the right circumstances, many different metals can detect radio waves. Have you ever heard of someone getting radio signals on the fillings in their teeth? Or on their braces? It can happen!

However, let's just stick to getting radio signals on a homemade radio. You could listen to your radio by hooking up a small earphone. But with an earphone, the signal would be *very* faint. Even in store-bought crystal-radio kits, you can hardly hear the radio sta-

tions you receive. That's why we suggest using your stereo amplifier to make the signal louder.

1 Start by making the coil for the radio. Use the point of a scissors to poke three holes in the empty film canister. One hole goes in the bottom. The second and third holes go on the side of the can, just ⅛" from the top and bottom, as shown in the drawing.

Now you want to wrap the 22-gauge hook-up wire around the film canister. But first, push the end of the wire through the side hole near the bottom of the film can, and then push it out the bottom hole. Pull out about 6" of wire and leave it dangling. Coil the rest of the wire *tightly* around the film can in

a single layer, until you have filled all the space up to the top hole. The wire must be tightly wrapped, with no spaces between the coils. There should be about 25 or 30 "turns" in your coil. Cut the wire, leaving about 1 foot extra. Push the end of the wire through the top hole and pull it tight. For now, leave the extra 1 foot of wire dangling.

2 Next you will make the radio's capacitor. Cut a 7" by 18" piece of corrugated cardboard from a carton. Try to cut the cardboard so that the ridges or corrugations are going *across* the short (7") side instead of up and down the 18" side. Measure up 8" from the long end, and draw a line. Use your scissors point to "score" (cut partway through) the cardboard along the line. Now you can easily fold the cardboard backward, along the line.

When the cardboard is folded, it will make a "pocket." You will want to line the pocket with a single piece of heavy-duty aluminum foil. The lining must also come outside the pocket and turn over onto the front of the pocket, as shown in the drawing. To do this, cut a piece of heavy-duty aluminum foil 6" wide and 17" long. Lay the cardboard flat and tape the foil to it with transparent tape, being sure to leave an inch or so hanging over the short end. Tape around all sides. Fold the foil over the short end and tape the edges down.

Fold the cardboard in half with the foil inside to form the pocket. The extra 1" of foil will show as a flap on the outside of the pocket. With masking tape, tape the

pocket closed along the edges, leaving the top of the pocket open. Try to tape the pocket together very tightly.

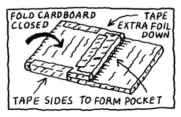

FOLD CARDBOARD CLOSED — TAPE EXTRA FOIL DOWN

TAPE SIDES TO FORM POCKET

3 Next you will need to make a "tuner." Cut an 8" by 10" piece of heavy-duty aluminum foil and put it between two pieces of 8½" by 11" typing paper to make a sandwich. Fold all three in half like a book. The book will be 5½" by 8½".

FOLD IN HALF LIKE A BOOK

PLACE 8x10" FOIL BETWEEN 2 SHEETS OF 8½x11" PAPER

4 Get ready to wire it all up! But first... you should practice stripping the insulation (the plastic coating) from the wire. For practice, use an extra piece of wire and your scissors. Cut very gently, until you have cut through the plastic *without* cutting the

copper wire. Slide the insulation off the end of the wire.

Use transparent tape to mount your coil on top of the cardboard pocket. Put it right next to the aluminum foil "flap."

Remember that you have two wires dangling out of the ends of the coil. One of them is 6" long. Strip off 4" of insulation from the end of this wire. Then tape it down *tightly* to the aluminum-foil flap.

The other dangling wire is about 12" long. Strip off 4" of insulation from the end of it. Now comes the hard part. You want to strip or bare a 1" section of this wire. With your scissors, gently cut through the insulation at a point about an inch or so from where it comes out of the film canister. But instead of pulling the plastic all the way off, just slide it down the wire about an inch. Let's call this the "bare spot."

Attach the *end* of the long dangling wire to the tuner "book" you made out of typing paper and foil. Slip the stripped end of the wire

into the book, near the crease, and tape it to the foil tightly.

TAPE SHORT WIRE TO FOIL FLAP AND LONG WIRE TO TUNER — TUNER — BARE SPOT

5 Cut a new piece of 22-gauge hook-up wire to be your antenna. The antenna should be about 30 feet long, although 20 feet is probably enough. Strip one end of the wire and attach it to the "bare spot" by twisting it around and around tightly.

Look at the phono cable. One end has two kinds of bare wires sticking out of it. Find the one that is in the center and has its own plastic insulation.

Now look at the diode and find the end that has a painted band around it. (It will probably be a black band or ring.) Connect the banded end of the diode to the center wire of the phono cable, by twisting them together tightly.

Attach the other end of the diode to the "bare spot" where the antenna has al-

LEAVE 1" EXTRA FOIL FOR FLAP — USE TRANSPARENT TAPE

FIND DIFFERENT STATIONS BY SLIDING THE TUNER UP & DOWN

1010
1050
1130

CLAMP POCKET TIGHT WITH CLOTHESPIN

ready been attached.

There is another wire—probably a twisted one—coming out of the phono cable. Tape it down tightly to the aluminum flap on the outside of the pocket.

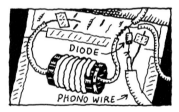

DIODE

PHONO WIRE

6 Slide the tuner—your paper-and-foil book—into the pocket. You will tune in different stations by sliding the tuner in and out.

To plug your radio into your stereo amplifier, first turn off the power. Turn the volume all the way off.

Unplug your phono turntable from the amplifier. Plug the phono cable from your crystal radio into that input jack. Or you can simply plug your crystal radio into an auxiliary input, if your amp has one.

Turn on the power and set your amplifier to the PHONO or AUX setting. Turn up the volume until you hear a little noise. Slide the crystal radio's tuner in and out of the pocket to find various radio stations. When you identify a station, you can draw a line on the tuner paper, and write down the station's call letters or frequency.

If you have trouble receiving stations, try pressing on the pocket with your fingers so the aluminum foil lining pieces come more closely together.

AFTERWORDS

It's easy to understand the principles of how a radio can be made out of coiled wire, foil, and cardboard.

One principle centers around the relationship between a coil and a capacitor, the two main parts of your crystal radio. A coil made out of copper wire can store magnetic energy. The aluminum-foil pocket capacitor can store electric energy. When you connect a coil to a capacitor, the magnetic energy in the coil flows toward the capacitor, and the electric energy in the capacitor flows toward the coil. The circuit formed by the two is called a tank circuit because it acts like a storage tank for energy.

But how does the energy—or the radio waves—get into the capacitor in the first place? Radio waves are electromagnetic. They don't travel on the air, like sound waves; they travel on themselves by oscillating between electric energy and magnetic energy.

When these radio waves hit your crystal radio's antenna, the electric part of the signal starts the electrons in the antenna moving back and forth. These electrons then produce a tiny electric field at the end of the wire. You'll notice that the end of your radio's antenna is attached to the same wire that goes into the tuner (the book). So the signal from the radio station is being delivered through the antenna to the tuner, which transfers that signal to the capacitor (the pocket). Now the radio waves are trapped, and all you need to do is change those radio waves into sound waves so you can hear them.

That's where the diode comes in. The diode allows energy to flow in one direction only. It sends the signal to your earphone or amplifier and speakers. Your speakers convert the signal to sound energy.

HOME MOVIES

HOME MOVIES

1 gal = 3.8 l	3 in = 7.6 cm
5 gal = 19 l	3 1/2 in = 8.9 cm
1/4 in = .64 cm	5 1/2 in = 14 cm
2 in = 5.1 cm	18 in = 45.7 cm
3 in x 5 in = 7.6 cm x 12.7 cm	

Lights, camera, action! You can be a big-time movie-maker by creating your own cartoons and movie "projector," in about 30 minutes.

YOU WILL NEED

1 Empty plastic 1-gallon jug
   (the kind that bleach or detergent comes in)
2 Tiny screw eyes
Ruler
Dark or black pen
   (Felt-tip type is best.)
Sharp pocket knife
   or utility knife
Several rubber bands
Cellophane tape
White paper
Thumbtack
Plain white 3″ × 5″
   index cards

When the lights go down at the Saturday movie matinee and the curtains slide open, an animated cartoon usually starts off the show. Or maybe your favorite cartoons are on TV on Saturday morning. Now you can have fun watching cartoons any day of the week, whenever you want. You can make your private movie studio and "screening room" at home — and learn how your eyes let you see pictures "move."

1 First soak or scrape any labels off the jug. Then draw 2 lines all the way around the jug — one about 3½″ from the bottom and the other about 5½″ from the bottom. Use a ruler, or try this: Stack up some books until they measure about 3½″ high; then lay your pen on top of the books and rotate the bottle carefully against the pen point. Add more books and repeat the process for the 5½″ line.

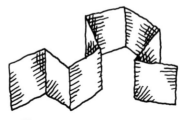

2 Cut a strip of paper several inches wide and exactly long enough to reach around the jug. Fold the strip in half, and in half again, and once again. When it is unfolded, you should see 8 equal segments.

3 Wrap the strip around the jug again (maybe tape it there) and make a mark on the jug at each paper fold, making sure that the marks are between the two lines at 3½″ and 5½″.

4 Use the knife to carefully cut a slot from line to line, ¼″ wide, at each of the marks you just made on the jug. Then cut the top *most of the way off,* just below the level of the handle. *Leave about 2″ uncut right below the handle.*

5 Screw one of the screw eyes into the center of the jug cap and the other screw eye into the center of the bottom. Your cartoon "projector" is now completed.

6 Next, cut several 3″ strips of paper just exactly long enough to form a loop that will fit *inside* the jug. (You might have to tape a few strips together to get the right length.) For most

PUSH LOOP DOWN TO BOTTOM

jugs, the size will be 18″ by 3″. Fold the strips into eighths, just as you did in Step 2. Copy one of the sample movie strips onto one of your paper strips. Form the strip into a circle, making sure that the drawings face the *inside,* and tape the loop ends together. Drop the loop into the jug and push it down to the bottom. Reattach the top of the jug to the bottom with strips of tape.

7 Using rubber bands tied together and attached to the screw eyes, suspend the jug between two points, above and below.

For instance, you can use a thumbtack to hang the jug from an open doorway, then put a chair underneath and attach the bottom of the jug to the chair's backrest. Then stand on the chair, turn the jug around a few times, and release it. Look into the jug through the rotating slots and watch your home-made cartoons move! That's *animation.*

8 Now that you have the equipment and the idea, make up some strips of your own. Everyone in the family can make up a cartoon or two. Here are some hints for success:

■ Start with a simple movement, like a ball bouncing up and down. Try to "see" the motion in your mind before you draw.
■ Be sure to break the movement down into several small steps so that the final motion will be smooth.

■ If parts of the picture should *not* move (like the outline of the face of a winking person), it's best to draw it once with a dark pen, and then trace that part on each section of the movie strip, or "frame." Now that part will appear to be motionless in the cartoon.

USE TACK TO SUSPEND JUG FROM DOORWAY AND ATTACH BOTTOM TO CHAIR. WIND UP JUG... THEN RELEASE IT!

Movie Show 1¢

COPY THESE SAMPLE MOVIES ON A STRIP 18″ × 3″.

VARIATIONS

■ Make up a bunch of blank paper strips and invite neighbors and friends in for an afternoon of cartoon making and viewing. Show some of your favorites to start off the show, and then teach the guests how to make their own.

■ Make a larger movie projector out of a 5-gallon bucket, a plastic wastebasket, or 5-gallon commercial ice-cream tub. With this larger container, you can cut *twice* as many slots and double the number of movements that you can put into your cartoon. What's the advantage? Longer features! And with more movements, your cartoons will have more realistic motions. Experiment with this new "feature-length" film studio.

■ There is another kind of homemade animated feature — the flip book. It works on the same basic optical and mechanical principles you've just learned. To make a flip book, you will need a pack or two of plain white 3" x 5" index cards. Staple about 30 to 35 together along one 3" edge. Draw a series of illustrations on the pages, and flip through the book at a medium speed. Now try a faster flip, and then a slower one. Which works better: the flip-book cartoons or the jug-theater cartoons?

AFTERWORDS

The movie machine you just made is a simple version of a device invented in the 19th century called a *kinetoscope*. The principles involved are very similar to those that apply to the modern-day movies that we all enjoy.

If you were to put one of your eight-frame cartoon strips inside of a transparent bottle and rotate it, all you would see is a blur. The key is to separate each image in some way so that your eye actually sees a series of single images in rapid succession. If the images flash quickly enough, one after another, our brain does not register the "dark" spaces between the images. In your bleach-jug kinetoscope, the "dark" spaces that separate the images are provided by the plastic sections between the slots you peek into.

The motion pictures that you see at the theater or at home rely on two inventions: the movie camera and the movie projector. The movie camera records individual, still images on a long strip of film, just like a snapshot camera does, except that a roll of movie film is much longer. The main difference is that a movie camera doesn't take just one shot and stop. It takes one picture after another as long as the shutter trigger is held down. Usually the camera records 24 pictures each second!

The other device that brings the motion picture to life is the projector. The projector uses a bright light to illuminate the images. Then a mechanism advances the film in front of the light and a shutter interrupts the beam of light after each individual image — 24 times each second. A lens focuses the images on a wall or special screen so you can view the movie.

The last phenomenon that makes the movies possible takes place in the human brain. The retina of the eye can retain an image briefly after it has gone from the screen. This "afterimage" dissolves into the next image that flashes on the screen, giving the illusion of smooth motion.

Specialized movie cameras can play time tricks on us, either speeding time up so that we can see things happen that normally take a long time, or slowing time down so that we can observe events that usually happen too rapidly to see. Would you like to see all the leaves on a maple tree turn bright autumn colors, and then fall off of the tree — all in a few minutes? Simply train your movie camera on the tree and expose one frame of film every 5 minutes during the daylight hours in the month of October. When you show the film at the usual 24 frames per second, you can see the whole fall drama in a matter of about 3 minutes!

For the slow-motion effect, you need a camera that can expose film at the rate of 240 frames per second. Then you can film the flight of a hummingbird for three seconds, capturing a total of 720 images. Projected at the standard rate of 24 frames per second, all those fancy wing beats that happen in three seconds can be slowed to fill 30 seconds. This is something that can't be seen with the human eye.

You won't be able to do all of these special effects at home, but your simple bleach-bottle kinetoscope is a good start. Next stop: Hollywood!

DRAWING MACHINE

DRAWING MACHINE

Here's a simple "drawing machine" you can make in one hour. Use it to copy a picture in any size you want!

YOU WILL NEED

Corrugated cardboard, about 20″ × 10″

2 or 3 Pieces of corrugated cardboard or 1 piece of plywood, each about 20″ square

White drawing paper or shelf paper

3 to 6 Paper clasps (small brass pins with rounded heads attached to two metal strips that can be bent back; strips must be at least 1″ long)

1 Thumbtack or pushpin

An awl or hand drill, tape, cutting knife or scissors, ruler

1 Pencil and 1 felt-tip pen or 2 soft-lead pencils

It's easy to *trace* a picture — but have you ever tried to copy one and make it larger or smaller? You may start off okay, but then maybe a line is too long or too short and you have to start all over again. With this drawing machine called a *pantograph,* you can have fun tracing a design or picture and watching a smaller or larger copy appear on the paper too!

1 Cut the corrugated 20″ × 10″ cardboard (from the top or bottom of a box) into 4 strips 11″ × 1¼″ and 4 strips 7″ × 1¼″. (It's okay if you make them a little wider.) Be careful with the cutting knife!

2 Divide the 11″ strips and the 7″ strips into sets of two strips each. On each strip, put a pencil mark ½″ in from one end; then put a mark every 2″, beginning from the first mark. You should have 6 marks on the 11″ strips, and 4 on the 7″ strips.

3 With an awl or hand drill make a hole at each mark on each strip. Then tightly tape each set of strips together, one on top of the other, to make 4 separate "drawing arms." Be sure you don't tape over the holes!

4 With a paper clasp, fasten the two longer strips together at the ½″ mark (Point A in the illustration). Fasten the other two 7″ strips to the long strips at Points B and C. That's your pantograph!

5 To make your drawing board, tape the large square pieces of corrugated cardboard together, one on top of the other; or just use the piece of plywood. Cover the drawing board over with paper to make a clean, flat working surface. With a thumbtack or pushpin, firmly anchor your pantograph to the drawing board at Point D.

6 Push your pencils into the holes at Points E and F. Be sure the pencil at Point E holds the two drawing arms together. If you have trouble, use a little tape to hold the pencil to the lower arm. (Don't tape the two arms together; they must be able to move.)

shifting. If you use the pencil at Point E to draw your design, the pencil at Point F will make a large copy of your design. If you use the pencil at Point F, the other pencil will make a smaller copy!

VARIATIONS

■ You can change the copy of your drawing just by adjusting the connections of the drawing arms. Experiment by moving the connection at Point B one hole closer to D. What happens to the copy of your drawing? It may look distorted — like something in a fun-house mirror! Next try attaching the short arms to different points on the long arms. Move the pencils to different points. Draw first with one pencil and then with the other. Can you figure out what happens when you make the changes?

■ You can also extend, or lengthen, your pantograph. (But then you will certainly need a larger drawing board!) You can add more arms too; cut a few extra 11" strips of cardboard in sets of twos taped together to make stiff drawing arms. Make the same holes as you made in the first set. Then attach your new arms and make two or three copies, adding more pencils.

■ The copies may come out too light if you use a lead pencil; why not try a colored felt-tip marker, the size of a pencil, on the copying arm instead?

■ If you have a favorite comic book character, you can use your pantograph to trace it in a different size. Put the picture on the drawing board, under your paper, and trace along the outline with the pencil at Point F. Is your copy larger or smaller than the original?

■ If you have a hand drill and a ³⁄₁₆" bit, you can use thin wooden strips of lath, instead of cardboard, for the drawing arms. You can even use cheap wooden rulers that you buy in the dimestore. You'll need at least three (cut one in half), but four would be ideal. Drill

7 Now you're ready to "draw double." Set your paper on the drawing board, under the pantograph. Tape each corner of the paper to prevent it from

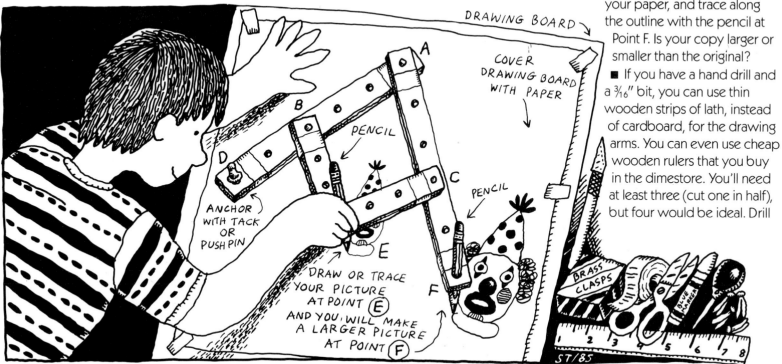

your holes and use paper clasps that are at least 1" or 1¼" long to attach the drawing arms.

Copying machines in an office may make copies faster, but it's much more fun to make your own pantograph and watch it make copies as you draw!

AFTERWORDS

Do your eyes ever play tricks on you? Perhaps — when a magician seems to pull a coin out of the air. But a pantograph plays no tricks on you when it enlarges or reduces a picture you draw or trace.

This change in size depends on the *ratio* of the distances between the tracing instrument (your pencil) and the drawing, or copying, instrument (the second pencil or felt-tip pen) to the pivot points (the points where the arms of the pantograph are attached). If the distance increases evenly — that is, if

points B and C in the drawing above are changed by the same amount — the copy will get bigger. Some pantographs will enlarge a drawing as much as 15 times its original size — a ratio of 15 to 1. By reversing the positions of the tracing and drawing instruments, you can make the picture smaller.

Interesting distortions can be made by changing the pivot points so that the arms are no longer parallel. For example, adjust the pivot point at A. Put the paper clasp through the first hole of one arm and the second or third hole of the other arm. If the tracing pencil draws a circle, the copying pencil will produce an oval or elipse. Trace a square and your copy will be a diamond!

Another way to enlarge a picture? Look at it through a magnifying glass! The glass is a double-convex lens, curved

out on both sides. It too relies on the relationship of distance to a point of contact, or *focal point*. But your eyes play a key part. We see an object because light rays bounce off of that object and into our eye (see diagram). As they pass through the *cornea,* then the *iris* (the colored part of your eye), the *pupil* (the black part),

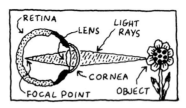

and the lens, the light rays are bent and brought together at the focal point of the *retina*. Strange as it seems, the image that is focused on the retina is *upside down* and *flat!* But by means of the many nerves to the brain, the image is processed into the correct image that we "see."

When we look through a magnifying glass, light rays bounce off the object, pass through the lens and are bent inward to meet at a point called the *focus* (see illustration #2). The distance from the center of the lens to the focus is the *focal length*. If the object (a word on a page, a leaf, or some other small item)

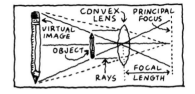

is less than one focal length from the lens, you will see an image that is right side up and larger than the original object.

Enlarging pictures with a pantograph or a magnifying glass can be fun. They work in different ways, but one thing never changes: The way your eyes work when they're *not* playing tricks on you!

1/2 in = 1.27 cm	3/16 in = .48 cm
1 in = 2.54 cm	2 in = 5.1 cm
2 in = 5.1 cm	7 in = 17.8 cm
11 in x 1 1/4 in = 27.9 cm x 3.2 cm	
20 in x 10 in = 50.8 cm x 25.4 cm	

WHISTLES AND FLUTES

WHISTLES AND FLUTES

You don't have to be able to sing to make beautiful music. All you need is about 45 minutes to set up this activity, a steady hand, a slide whistle, and a lungful of air. Get ready …get set…BLOW!

YOU WILL NEED

Coping saw or small tubing cutter (see Note)
1 Length of ½″ diameter copper tubing (see Note)
Ruler
Pencil
Fine sandpaper
1 Dowel, 7″ long with a diameter large enough to fit snugly inside the copper tubing
Hammer
Nail
Pliers
Cloth tape or masking tape
Various empty soda bottles
Note: Inexpensive copper tubing and tubing cutter can be easily obtained from a do-it-yourself home-improvement center or from some hardware stores.

Did you ever wish you could play a slide trombone? How about trying out the next best thing: the slide whistle? Just like a trombone, a slide whistle comes complete with all the notes on the musical scale at your fingertips.

SLIDE WHISTLE

1 Cut an 8″ length of copper tubing, using the coping saw. Or follow the directions on the tubing cutter and use it to cut the pipe.

2 Place a piece of fine sandpaper on the floor, rough-side up. Rub the cut ends of the copper tube back and forth over the sandpaper to sand the "burrs," or rough edges, off. This is the best way to sand, because it keeps the ends of the tube *flat*. Flat ends will produce the

1/2 in = 1.27 cm
3 in = 7.6 cm
7 in = 17.8 cm
8 in = 20.3 cm

MOVE PIPE IN UPRIGHT POSITION TO KEEP ENDS FLAT—
SANDPAPER

best whistle and flute sounds. Use another piece of sandpaper to smooth the outside and inside edges of the tube, so that you can put your mouth up to the pipe without hurting yourself. Now try it. Can you blow *across* the top of the pipe and make a sound? Put your thumb or palm on the bottom of the pipe to *completely* close the bottom hole and try again. Practice blowing until you get a clear, strong tone.

HAMMER A NAIL PART WAY INTO END
NAILS

3 Sand the ends of the wooden dowel if they are rough. Then hammer a nail partway into the end of the dowel. Use pliers to bend the nail into a hook shape. The bent nail is your handle for the slide part of the whistle.

4 Insert the dowel into the copper tube and blow, while moving the slide up and down. If you don't get a clear tone, it is because the dowel doesn't fit tightly enough. Remove the dowel and wrap it with a layer of cloth tape or masking tape. Try it again. Keep adding layers of tape until the dowel fits snugly enough to close the tube completely. At first you might not have enough tape, and then you might have too much. But keep trying until the fit is right. Can you play a scale by stopping the slide in various positions?

WARM UP YOUR WHISTLE

The best warm-up for slide-whistle blowing is the always popular "soda bottle full of water" trick. Gather up four or five empty soda bottles. (Plastic ones are okay.) Add some water to the first one so that it is about ¼ full, fill the second bottle ½ full, and so on. Each bottle should have a different amount of water in it.

To blow, pull your lips in tightly against your teeth so that both lips are kind of flat. Your top lip should stick out just a tiny bit farther than your bottom lip. Hold the mouth of the bottle *firmly* against your lower lip, and blow *across* the opening—not *into* it! Try to make some of your breath hit the *far inside edge* of the bottle mouth, while most of your breath glides out across the top.

What makes the bottle with the most water give you the highest tone? Is it the water, the size of the bottle, the size of the bottle opening—or something else? For the answer, try experimenting with different-size bottles, each filled with exactly 3 inches of water. (Or, if you can't figure it out, check out the information in the Afterwords!)

FILL EACH SODA BOTTLE WITH A DIFFERENT AMOUNT OF WATER—

AFTERWORDS

If you've ever plucked a guitar and watched the strings go *boinnnng,* or put your hand on a drum while it was being played, or stood close enough to a gong to *feel* the sound hit your chest—you know that *vibrations* make sounds. But what's the difference between ordinary sounds and *music*? The answer is that the vibrations in music are very regular and even. The vibrations that create nonmusical sounds are not.

Here's one way to show yourself the difference between musical sounds and nonmusical sounds. First sing the word "hair" in any note and hold it for 10 seconds. Now try to say the word "hair" very evenly, and take 10 seconds to do it. But here's the catch: Don't let your voice go up or down. You must *speak,* not sing, the word without letting your voice change its tone at all. You'll find that it can't be done! If you really keep your speaking voice that steady and even, it turns into singing!

So the difference between talking and singing has to do with the steady, regular vibrations of your vocal cords. But what vibrates in a slide whistle or flute? Is it the metal itself? No. The sound you hear when you play your slide whistle comes from the column of air inside the tube. As your breath hits the inside edge opposite your lip, it starts the column of air vibrating.

You can test this by making two single pipes: one of plastic and one of metal or rubber hose. If they are both the same length, they will both produce the same note—although one may have a mellower sound and the other may have a shrill quality.

Modern-day flutes, of course, are just one long pipe with all the notes in the scale. To play a low note, the flute player must cover all the holes, so that the column of air is very long. To shorten the column of air, the flute player simply opens one of the holes. That lets the air "escape" sooner than it would have in the longer pipe.

Believe it or not, the flute's closest relative is the organ. In fact, an early flute called a pan-pipe is said to have inspired

the invention of a water organ in the third century B.C. Organs make music when air is forced across the openings of pipes; so technically that makes them wind instruments. But if you've ever seen the size of the pipes on an organ, you'll be glad you don't have to blow into them to make them play!

All musical instruments make music using the same principles. To produce a note, something must vibrate and the shorter it is, the higher the note. A piano has short strings for high notes and long strings for low notes. But violins have only four strings and they all seem to be the same length. How do you get high notes on a violin? The musician shortens the string—or really shortens the length a string can vibrate—by holding the string tightly against the neck of the violin with his or her fingers.

If you've ever wondered how the air in a trumpet can be made shorter or longer, just look at all those twists and turns in the tubing. The valves on a trumpet open and close

certain sections of tubing to change the overall length. On a slide trombone, you can *see* how the tubing is made longer. Just like on your slide whistle, the slide moves in and out to change the length of the column of air. On trumpets and trombones, something else vibrates too: the player's lips!

TIME OUT

TIME OUT

8 in = 20.3 cm   40 ft = 12.2 m
1 C = .24 l   59 ft = 17.9 m
16 oz = 480 m l

Got a minute? Great—but you'll need more than that to make the timekeepers in this timely activity. Allow about 15 minutes to set up each "clock"—and then plan to *watch* them (excuse the pun) for an hour or so!

YOU WILL NEED

An 8″ piece of cotton string
Vegetable oil
Heavy-duty aluminum foil or pie pan
Matches
A watch or stopwatch
2 Identical straight-sided candles (not tapers)
Candlesticks (or Plasticine, or modeling clay, to hold candles upright)
Small nail
Empty milk carton
Ballpoint pen
5 Identical paper or Styrofoam cups
Large cardboard box
Brass paper fasteners (with a head and two prongs)
Empty jar
2 Small plastic soda bottles
Heavy-duty tape
Box of table salt

When the ref calls "Time out!"—how does he know when to call "Time in?" He uses his stopwatch, of course. These days we have lots of timekeepers—from digital watches to Big Ben, London's famous clock tower. But in ancient times, finding ways to measure time was a problem. How could a peasant bake bread if he didn't know how long to leave it in the oven? Here are some clocks, timers, and stopwatches that were used a long, long time ago. Make them all and then compare: Which clock is the most accurate? Which one would you use if you really wanted to be on time?

A String Timer

Cut a piece of cotton string 8″ long. Knot the string at every inch, trying to keep the spaces between the knots equal. Pour a small amount of vegetable oil in a small dish and soak the string in the oil. Lay the oily string on an aluminum pie pan or on a piece of heavy-duty aluminum foil with the edges turned up. Place the aluminum pan in the kitchen sink for safety.

Have an adult help with the next step. Light one end of the string and let it burn on the aluminum pan. Make sure the aluminum pan is lying flat—or with the lighted end of the string slightly uphill. Otherwise the string won't burn evenly.

How long does it take for the string to burn from one knot to the next? Time it with a watch or stopwatch. How long does an 8″ string burn?

KNOT STRING AT EVERY INCH

A Candle Timer

Place two identical straight-sided candles in candlesticks. Or set them side by side on an aluminum pie pan and hold the candles in place with small blobs of Plasticine or modeling clay. Ask an adult's help to light one of the candles. ***Be sure to keep your hair and clothing away from the flame.*** Let the candle burn for exactly 10 minutes. Blow out the flame. How far has it burned? Hold the first candle next to the other one. Use a nail to scratch a ring around the other candle to show how far down it will burn in 10 minutes. Continue scratching rings, equally spaced, around the candles. Each mark represents 10 minutes. Light one of the candles again and burn three sections. Time the Candle Timer. How accurate was it? Did the three 10-minute sections burn for 30 minutes? Which clock is more accurate: the String Timer or the Candle Timer?

A Water Timer

Open up the top of an empty milk carton and rinse it. Use a ballpoint pen to mark equally spaced lines on the inside of the carton. Poke a small hole in the side of the carton, about an inch from the bottom.

Fill the carton with water and let the water run out the hole into the sink. How long does it take for the water to go down from the top line

to the next line? Is the emptying time between each line the same? Or does the water empty more slowly as it drains? Is this an accurate clock?

USE A NAIL TO SCRATCH RINGS

USE A BALL POINT PEN TO MARK EQUALLY SPACED LINES ON THE INSIDE OF CARTON

POKE A HOLE IN BOTTOM OF 5 IDENTICAL STYROFOAM CUPS AND FASTEN IN A ROW ONE ABOVE EACH OTHER

SCRATCH AROUND OTHER CANDLE

CLOCK

ST/88

REYNOLDS PASTEURIZED AND HOMOGENIZED MILK

SPOUT TO OPEN

MILK

PASTEURIZED HOMOGENIZED VITAMIN D

ONE QUART

POKE A HOLE ABOUT ONE INCH FROM BOTTOM

WEIGHT INSIDE OF BOX WITH BOOKS OR ROCKS

USE BRASS PAPER FASTENER TO FASTEN CUPS TO SIDE OF BOX.

TURN OVER TO START TIMER

TAPE CAPS TOGETHER W/ HEAVY TAPE

POKE A SMALL HOLE W/ NAIL

ORANGE DRINK

DIAMOND SALT

A Deluxe Water Timer

Poke one hole in the bottom of each of 5 identical paper or Styrofoam cups. Fasten the cups in a row, one above the other, to the outside of a cardboard box. To fasten them, use brass paper fasteners poked through the cups and the box. Weight the inside of the box with rocks or books, so it won't tip over. Put an empty jar under the bottom cup to catch the water.

Measure out one full cup of water and pour it into the top cup. How long does it take the water to run through each cup? How long to reach the bottom? Repeat the experiment and time it carefully. Is the Deluxe Water Timer more accurate or less accurate than the other clocks you have made?

An Hourglass—or a 3-Minute Timer?

Wash and completely dry the insides of two small plastic soft-drink bottles. (The 16-ounce size works best.) Remove both caps and use heavy-duty tape to tape them together with their top sides touching. Use a nail to poke a small hole straight through both bottle caps. Fill one bottle three-fourths full of ordinary table salt. Screw on the double lid. Turn the other bottle upside down on top of the one filled with salt. Screw it to the double cap. To start your timer, simply turn it over and watch the salt run from the top bottle to the bottom. How long does it take? You might want to adjust the amount of salt in the timer so that it takes exactly 3 minutes for the salt to run out.

Which of the clocks that you made is the most reliable and accurate?

AFTERWORDS

What's the biggest clock in the world? According to the *Guinness Book of World Records,* you have your choice. The biggest clock *face*—the floral clock in Hokkaido, Japan—is more than 59 feet in diameter. The most *massive* clock is located in the Cathedral of St. Pierre in Beauvais, France. And the largest four-faced clock, with each face 40 feet in diameter, is on the building of the Allen-Bradley Co. in Milwaukee, Wisconsin.

But hold on a second… and look down. You're actually *standing on* the biggest timekeeper known to man. Earth, as it goes around the sun, is the "clock" that tells us when it's day or night, when it's summer, winter, spring, or fall. All of the other clocks and timepieces we use are designed to measure—and to put a name or a number on—the chunks of time we experience. But for centuries, people had no better way to tell time than to look up at the position of the sun in the sky. But it's not so easy to measure out smaller segments of time—like an hour—by simply

looking up. That's why people invented clocks.

Perhaps the oldest clock known is the sundial, which was invented more than 4,000 years ago. Water and candle clocks too, while not as ancient as the sundial, are very early clocks. The Greeks used water clocks called *clepsydras,* which means "thief of water," to time speeches made by lawyers during trials. Judges wanted to be sure that each lawyer was given the same amount of time to plead a case. Another timekeeper used in the courts was the hourglass full of sand. Each person was allowed to speak until the sand (time) ran out from the upper chamber into the lower chamber—thus the expression "time is running out"!

One of the biggest advances in the measurement of time started in a church in 1581. Seventeen-year-old Galileo Galilei became bored with the church service and started watching the swinging lights hanging overhead. He noticed that no matter how far the lights swung, they always seemed to take the same amount of

time to complete a swing. He used his own pulse to time the swings. Galileo figured that anything that moved in such a regular way could probably be used to measure time. Later on, pendulum clocks were invented. These clocks use a weight that falls slowly to give small pulses of energy to each swing. However, a swinging weight in a clock is of no use to a ship tossing at sea. So in 1761, John Harrison invented a wind-up clock that was accurate.

Today, we have many very accurate timekeepers—so your candle clock is rather out of date. Quartz-crystal timepieces, which were invented in the 1920s, are accurate to within $\frac{1}{1,000}$ of a second each 6 months. Atomic clocks, invented in the 1950s, are even more accurate. In fact, the world's *most* accurate clock is an atomic clock in the U.S. Naval Research Laboratory in Washington, D.C. It would take 1.7 *million* years for this clock to gain or lose one second! By the way, what time *is* it?

3-D VIEWER

3-D VIEWER

2 in = 5.1 cm	12 in = 30.5 cm
2 1/2 in = 6.4 cm	24 in = 60.9 cm
6 in = 15.2 cm	4 ft = 1.2 m
11 in = 27.9 cm	5 ft = 1.5 m
8 1/2 in x 11 in = 22 cm x 27.9 cm	

Take a look into the third dimension—with this fantastic 3-D Viewer! You can use your own camera to take the pictures. After the pictures are developed, you'll need about 20 minutes to make the viewer.

YOU WILL NEED

A camera
Print film for your camera
Tape measure or yardstick
Cardboard tube at least 2" in
    diameter and 24" long
    (or you can use two
    tubes, each 12" long)
Scissors
Felt-tip marker or pen
Pencil
Transparent tape

Years ago, 3-D Viewers were called *stereoscopes.* Each stereoscope held two pictures of the same scene. But each picture was taken from a slightly different point of view. Normally when you look at a photograph, you see only two dimensions: height and width—a flat image. But if you looked at one picture with one eye and the other picture with the other eye through a stereoscope, you would see an eye-popping 3-D scene—one with height, width, *and* depth. You can easily make a 3-D viewer that will transform your own photographs into amazingly lifelike scenes. But don't forget to buy extra film because there's a trick to it: You've got to photograph everything twice!

EXPERIMENT WITH YOUR EYES

Before you make your 3-D Viewer, you should find out a little bit about how you see. First, measure the distance between your eyes. If you are a grown-up (but not a *giant!*), your eyes are probably about 2½" apart, maybe a little less. Do you think each eye sees the same thing? Find out by holding up one finger in front of your face, about 6" away. Close your right eye and observe where your finger seems to be. Line your finger up with something vertical, like a doorway. Then open your right eye and close the left. Your finger will seem to "jump" back and forth, from one side of the doorway to the other. That's because you are seeing your finger differently, depending on which eye you use. Your right eye and your left eye see two different "pictures," from two different angles. When your brain puts the two pictures together, you see things three-dimensionally.

TAKING 3-D PICTURES

Please read all of the instructions below, *before* you begin photographing. That way you will be sure to get good results.

You can use any ordinary camera to take 3-D pictures. Simply load your camera and go outside on a fairly bright day. The idea is to take two pictures of the same scene, separated by about 2½", since that's the way your eyes see.

There are two good ways to take 3-D pictures. Method No. 1 is very easy. You simply hold the camera up to your right eye and take the picture. Then, for the second picture in the set, you hold the camera up to your left eye. This will automatically move the camera about 2½" to the left. If you use this method, you must hold your head very still between the two pictures, so that your angle of view doesn't change.

For Method No. 2, you put the camera on a table or another solid surface. Put a tape measure or yardstick behind the camera, parallel to it. Take your first picture, then move the camera exactly 2½" to the left. Now take the second picture. Again, you must be sure that the camera isn't twisted or turned between pictures.

HINTS FOR SUCCESS

■ Be sure to photograph every scene twice!

■ 3-D pictures work best if the different objects in the picture are at different distances from the camera. For instance, you might have a bicycle in the foreground. There could be some trees about 4' behind the bicycle. The sky would be your distant background.

■ Don't put the main subject *too* close to the camera lens. The main subject should be at least 5' away from the camera.

■ Remember that the subject and the background must remain exactly the same for both pictures. If you are photographing a street scene, be sure to take the second picture quickly—before a car moves, for instance—so that the street scene will be unchanged. If you are photographing a person, he or she must remain perfectly still for both pictures. Don't let your subject smile in Picture 1 and then frown in Picture 2!

■ The pictures you take will need to be cut so that they fit in the 3-D Viewer. Only part of each picture will be used. Remember this when you are composing your scene. Try to keep all of the important elements in the center of the "frame," or camera viewfinder.

MAKING THE 3-D VIEWER

You will need to start with a long cardboard tube, like the ones used to hold gift-wrapping paper. It should be at least 2" in diameter and at least 24" long. Cut the tube into two pieces, each 12" long. (If the tube is longer, cut off the extra length and discard it.) With a marker or pen, label one tube LEFT and the other one RIGHT.

If you don't have a cardboard tube, you can use stiff white paper. Use two sheets of paper, 8½" × 11". Roll each one into an 11" tube that is 2" in diameter.

Now hold the tubes up to your eyes and look toward a light. If the tubes are not held closely together, you will see two circles of light at the ends. But if the tubes are held tightly together at the far end, and *just slightly* separated at your eyes, the two circles of light will come together. You will be looking through two tubes, but seeing only one circle. Good! Now you know how to hold the tubes when you are viewing in 3-D.

VIEWING THE 3-D PICTURES

Remember that you photographed each scene or subject twice.

Find a set of two developed prints and look to make sure they are slightly different. You will notice that in one picture you can see a little more of the right side of the scene—or more of the right side of the *background*. That picture goes on the RIGHT tube. The other picture, showing more of the left, goes on the LEFT tube. Put both pictures, face up, together like a sandwich, and set them down on a flat surface. Stand one of the

LEFT PICTURE

RIGHT PICTURE

↑ MARK THE TUBES LEFT AND RIGHT

YOU CAN USE YOUR CAMERA TO TAKE 3-D PICTURES

tubes up on the main part of the picture and, using a pencil, trace around the outside of the tube.

Now cut out the circle from the pictures, cutting right through both prints at once. You will then have two circular photographs, each a little bit larger than the diameter of the tubes. Tape the right picture to the RIGHT tube and the left picture to the LEFT tube, with the pictures facing in.

Hold the tubes together and face a light source. At first, you might see two images or pictures. But slowly, the two pictures will *converge* in your mind, and you will see only one—just as you saw only one circle of light. Be patient. Sometimes it takes a minute or so for your mind to bring the two pictures together. When they do come together, you will see that your main subject stands out from the background in a very three-dimensional way!

AFTERWORDS

Hold on to your seats, horror fans. Here comes a hideously disfigured man in a black cape, with a face that looks like it's been through a three-alarm fire. (It has!) He's about to thrust his gnarled hand out at you, but you're not frightened, are you? After all—it's only a movie, isn't it? But wait! This movie is called *House of Wax*, and it's the most famous 3-D movie ever. When the hideous hand first came out of the movie screen in 1953, it looked so real that audiences all over America screamed.

To understand 3-D, you have to understand first that your eyes see separately and that your brain fuses the two images together. You can prove that with your cardboard tubes. Hold just one tube up to your right eye. Hold your left hand, palm open and facing you, next to the far end of the tube. Perhaps for a second, you will see two separate images: the hole in the end of the tube, and your hand beside it. But quickly your mind will force the two pictures to merge. Then, bingo! You'll be looking at a hole in the middle of your hand!

When you look around the room, your eyes see two slightly different pictures and your brain fuses them together. The two pictures you see are flat, *not* three-dimensional. It's only when those two flat views become one that you can actually see in three dimensions. Now you might cover one eye, look around, and say, "Everything looks three-dimensional to me." But in fact, you are being guided by other visual cues: the relative size of objects, shadows, and your past experience.

In truth, the world looks flat when viewed through only one eye—or through only one camera lens. But with two lenses, mounted side by side and about 2½" apart, two pictures can be taken at once—in just the way your eyes take two "pictures" at once. That's how stereo photography was born. In the 1800s, special cameras were designed with two lenses, and special viewing devices, *stereoscopes*, were invented.

Then for many years 3-D viewing went out of fashion. And it didn't come back until the 1950s—when television was invented. You see, people stopped going to the movies because they were too busy watching the tube. So Hollywood came up with 3-D films to draw audiences out to the theater again. As with stereo photography, 3-D movies were made by shooting two versions of the same scene—by strapping two huge movie cameras together. On one camera, a filter "polarized" the light horizontally. The other camera had a vertical polarizing filter. The two versions of the film were projected simultaneously and people in the audience viewed the movie through 3-D glasses with corresponding polarizing filters. That way, the left eye was allowed to see only one version of the film, and the right eye was allowed to see the other version. Again, the brain would fuse the two pictures.

So why aren't 3-D movies all the rage today? *Eye strain.* Although 3-D viewing is exciting, it can produce headaches after a while. For that reason, you'll want to go easy on the 3-D Viewer you made.

KALEIDOSCOPE

KALEIDOSCOPE

1/4 in = .64 cm	3 in = 7.6 cm
1 in = 2.54 cm	6 in = 15.2 cm
1 1/2 in = 3.8 cm	12 in = 30.5 cm

For at least 150 years, kaleidoscopes have been turning out many beautiful patterns. With two mirrors and some bits of plastic, you can create some colorful images of your own in about 1 hour.

YOU WILL NEED

2 or 3 Identical mirrors, any size between 1½" to 3" wide and 6" to 12" long (You can get these from a glass shop; tell the salesperson what you are making and ask to have the mirrors' edges polished. If the glass shop doesn't polish the edges of the mirrors, you will also need some fine sandpaper, emery cloth, or an emery board, and a small block of wood.)

Glass cleaner
Tissues
Pencil
Ruler
Some strips of cardboard larger than your mirrors
Scissors
Black construction paper or black tempera paint
Quick-drying glue
Masking tape
1 Clear plastic notebook divider or a clear plastic food container lid
Scraps of colored plastic or unwanted color film slides, or confetti
1 Translucent food container lid (one that you can see light through, but you can't see through completely)

1 Safety first! If the edges of your mirrors are not polished, handle them *very carefully* and polish them yourself. Wrap some fine sandpaper or emery cloth around a small block of wood and *carefully* sand the sharp edges and corners. Or you can use an emery board (you won't need the wood block) to do the same thing. When the edges are smooth and safe enough to be handled, clean the mirrors with glass cleaner.

2 Now, before you make your kaleidoscope, try these mirror experiments to find out how kaleido-

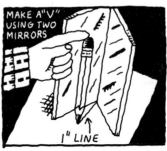

scopes work. Draw a line about 1" long on a piece of paper. Stand your two mirrors on their edges and make a "V" shape around the line, with one end of the line touching the point of the "V," as shown. What seems to happen to the line? Stand a pencil at the other end of the line. How many images of the pencil can you see? Change the angle between the mirrors — make the "V" wider or narrower — and see how many images are formed.

3 Cut a piece of heavy cardboard to measure about 1" wider than the mirrors you are using, and just as long. Cover the cardboard with black construction paper and glue it in place. Or use black tempera paint

to make one side of the cardboard black.

4 Now decide how big an angle — how wide a "V" — you want your kaleidoscope to have. (As you found in Step 2, you can vary the number of reflected images by changing the angle.) Make sure the shiny sides of the mirrors are *facing* each other, and tape two long sides of your mirrors together in the "V" shape you want.

5 Measure the widest distance across the opening between the two mirrors. Trim the width of the black cardboard so that it measures the same as the opening between the mirrors. Tape the cardboard to the mirrors with the black side facing *in*, forming a three-sided "tube." You may need a friend to help you hold the three pieces while you tape them. Wrap the tape around as shown in the diagram.

BLACK SIDE OF CARDBOARD FACES IN

6 Cover one open end of the tube with a clear triangle of plastic cut from a notebook divider or food-container lid. Secure it in place with fast-drying glue and tape—but don't let too much tape show on the plastic.

CLEAR PLASTIC FROM NOTEBOOK DIVIDER

7 Measure and cut three pieces of heavy cardboard, each one ¼" wider and longer than the

RUSSEL '87

↑ USE TAPE TO ATTACH OTHER ↗ TWO CARDBOARD COVERS

triangular tube. These will be the covering for your kaleidoscope. Attach them to the outside of the tube so that they stick out ¼" beyond the plastic-covered end of the tube. **Important:** Don't put glue on the backs of your mirrors. You can glue one cardboard cover to the black cardboard side of the tube, and then *use tape* to attach the other two cardboard covers.

8 Cut some pieces of unwanted color film slides or transparent colored plastic into small

PIECES OF COLORED PLASTIC OR FILM

shapes. You can also use confetti. Stand your kaleidoscope on end, with the clear plastic window facing up. Put about a dozen of these pieces on top of the clear window.

9 Find a "frosted" lid from a food container —one that lets light through, but that you can't see through completely. Cut a triangle of this plastic just big enough to cover the end of the tube. With the confetti and colored bits still in place on the clear window, place the frosted window on top of them. Glue or tape it in place. The confetti is now sandwiched between the frosted window and the clear window.

GLUE "FROSTED" TRIANGLE FROM FOOD CONTAINER LID

10 Finally, cut a triangle of heavy cardboard big enough to cover the other end of the kaleidoscope, and make a peephole in it about as wide as a pencil and off-center — closer to one corner than the others. Glue and tape this triangle in place, with the peephole closest to point of the "V" made by the mirrors.

PUT PEEPHOLE CLOSEST TO "V" MADE BY MIRRORS

11 Aim your kaleidoscope at a light (*not* direct sunlight) and look through the peephole. What do you see? Turn your scope slowly as you look at the light. What are your chances of seeing the same pattern twice?

VARIATION

■ If you want to try the deluxe kaleidoscope model, use a third mirror instead of the black cardboard floor.

AFTERWORDS

Your kaleidoscope is similar to one designed and patented by a Scottish physicist, Sir David Brewster, in 1817. Brewster's invention was so popular he sold more than 200,000 of them in the first few months. Brewster also came up with an even more fascinating version: a kaleidoscope with a convex lens mounted in the end instead of the plastic bits and confetti. Viewed through this device, the whole world becomes a series of symmetrical patterns, and even the plainest images look like blossoming flowers!

But kaleidoscopes can be more than toys. Until recently, a designer might use a kaleidoscope to create new patterns for such things as fabrics, carpets, and wallpaper. Now, however, designers more often use a computer to do the same job.

Your kaleidoscope also demonstrates some physical concepts, such as *opacity:* the ability of a substance to block out light. If you hold a piece of plywood between yourself and a burning candle, you won't see the candle *or* the light coming from the flame. That's because plywood is *opaque:* It doesn't let any light or sight through.

The opposite of opaque is *transparent.* Ordinary window glass is a good example of a transparent material. If you hold a piece of glass between you and the candle, you can see not only the light coming from the candle, but also the details of the candle's shape, size, color, and position. Transparent materials let light and sight through.

But what happens when you look at a burning candle through a sheet of waxed paper? You can see *some* light coming from the candle — certainly enough to tell whether or not the candle is lit. But you can't see any of the details. Waxed paper is a good example of a *translucent* material: It lets through some light, but not sight. How many other examples of translucent substances can you name? How would you describe the opacity of a glass of milk? The glass just after you finish drinking the milk?

Another principle at work in your kaleidoscope involves the *reflection* of light. First of all, light tends to travel in straight lines. Light entering a mirror in a straight line will reflect off the mirror in a straight line. But if the light hits the mirror at an angle, it will bounce off the mirror in the *opposite* direction, but at the same angle. This is the law of reflection: The angle going in has to equal the angle coming out. You can test this law by standing in front of a mirror that is only *half* as tall as you are. Surprisingly, you will be able to see your *whole* body, even though the mirror does not seem to be tall enough to do that job.

Most kaleidoscopes use about a 60-degree angle, which produces a six-sided pattern. Each side is an equal "slice" of the circle. The smaller the angle, the more images it creates. For instance, mirrors angled at 45 degrees will reflect eight equal images. You can figure out how many images you'll see with any given angle by measuring the angle with a compass and dividing the size of the angle into 360 — the number of degrees in a full circle. But as you probably noticed, *too* many repeated images can look too confusing. So cut down on the number of "slices" in your kaleidoscope pie!

SOLAR COOKER

SOLAR COOKER

8 in = 20.3 cm
14 in = 35.6 cm
3 ft = .9 m

If it's so hot outside you're *roasting,* stop! Don't let the sun roast *you.* Let it roast hot dogs and marshmallows instead! It will take about 45 minutes to cook up your own sun-powered ovens.

YOU WILL NEED
Empty mixing bowl
Aluminum foil
Flexible piece of cardboard about 8" by 14"
Piece of string 3 feet long
Scissors
Empty round oatmeal box, with lid
Marshmallows
3 long forks or long, pointed sticks
Hot dog

Did you know that on a clear day the summer sunshine is actually hot enough to cook meat outdoors? It's true. And the yukky truth: When you sit in the sun trying to get a tan, you're really cooking your own skin!

No one wants a roasted kid for lunch, so wear sunscreen when you're outside for long periods on a bright summer's day. (And don't be fooled by cloudy weather: The sun's rays can still penetrate and leave you with a bad burn.) Instead, let the sun go to work cooking a really delicious lunch — hot dogs and marshmallows prepared in your very own solar cooker!

1 You can make three different solar cookers and then have a marshmallow-roasting race to see which one works fastest. For the first solar cooker, all you need to do is line the inside of a large mixing bowl with aluminum foil, shiny-side up. (You may want to try two or three different bowls to see which one works best.)

2 For the second solar cooker, you need a piece of cardboard thin enough to bend. (The backing from a legal pad works well.) Cover one side of the cardboard with aluminum foil — again, shiny-side up. Then bend the cardboard into a semi-circle, with the foil on the inside of the curve. Use string to tie the cardboard in this position, as shown. This is easier to do if you wrap the string around twice and tie the knot in back.

3 Solar cooker No. 3 is really a hot-dog cooker, but you can also use it in the Great Marshmallow Toasting Race. To make the cooker, cut a long window in the side of an empty cylindrical oatmeal box. Line the inside of the box with aluminum foil. (Don't forget to put the shiny side up!)

4 Now it's cook-out time! But before you go outside, remember these rules: **Never look directly into the sun!** And be careful with the concentrated spots of sunlight your solar cooker will gather. Concentrated sunlight can burn your skin. **Also, don't look directly at any glaring or bright spot on your solar cooker.**

Outside, set your three solar cookers in a bright, sunny spot. Try to aim them so that the sun is falling directly on the foil. Then put one marshmallow on the end of each long stick or fork — and the race is on! The trick to toasting the marshmallows is to find out where the reflected sun's rays are crisscrossing. For each cooker, this hot spot will be in a different place.

Hold your hand over the bowl, and bring it down

THE GREAT MARSHMALLOW ROASTING RACE

1. LINE INSIDE OF BOWL WITH ALUMINUM FOIL

2. COVER ONE SIDE OF CARDBOARD WITH FOIL AND BEND USING STRING

3. LINE INSIDE OF OATMEAL BOX WITH FOIL AND CUT A LONG WINDOW

REMINDER: ALWAYS USE ALUMINUM FOIL SHINY SIDE UP!

43

slowly into the bowl until you find the hot spot. **But don't leave your hand there for more than a few seconds!**

For the bent cardboard cooker, you will probably find the hot spot somewhere near the center of the string — or just inside the string, closer to the foil.

The hot-dog cooker is designed to hold a hot dog on a stick *inside* the oatmeal box. So put your marshmallow on a stick and hold it in the center of the box.

Which cooker won the race? Can you figure out why one cooker works better than another?

AFTERWORDS

The sun gives out a fantastic amount of energy each day. If you could gather up all the fuel on Earth — all the gas, oil, and coal — and burn it fast enough to give off as much heat as we get from the sun, all of the fuel would be used up in three days.

Fortunately, we are not about to use up all of the fuel on Earth in three days. But Americans do use about 2,000 times as much energy today as the Colonists used in 1776. This is partly because the population has grown quite a bit since then, and partly because we continue to require more and more energy. We use about 25% of our energy to run cars and another 25% at home, for heating and electricity. Industry uses about 20% in manufacturing steel, automobiles, and other consumer goods. And that still leaves 30% — and guess where that goes? Into *making* energy! After all, it takes fuel to do things like mine coal, drill for oil, and transport raw materials to the refineries.

Strange as it may seem, all of the fuels on Earth come from the sun in one way or another. Here's how it works: Plants use the sun's energy to make their own food. Animals and people eat the plants. When plants, animals, and people die, the decaying process eventually — after millions of years — produces what we call fossil fuels: coal, gas, and oil. They were formed from pressure and heat on dead plant and animal remains. Indirectly, the sun has provided all of the energy we use.

But now that we are using so much more energy, some experts estimate that all of our gas, oil, and coal will be gone within 500 years. That's why people are turning to solar energy as an important alternative. Several different ways were developed to harness the sun's power and put it to work on Earth. Your solar cooker demonstrated one method: *concentrating* the sun's rays into a smaller area. This is a great technique for cooking, but to heat a large area like a house or swimming pool, it's more efficient to *collect* the sun's energy and store it until you need it. Maybe you've seen houses with solar panels on the roof. First the sun warms the panels up. Then the hot panels warm up some pipes just underneath the panels. Liquid in the pipes flows down into the house and warms a tank of water. A fan blows the warmth from the water into the air ducts to heat the house.

The biggest problem with solar collectors, like the roof panels, is that the sun has to be shining for them to work. On Earth, the sun isn't always visible. But out in space, the sun is always burning bright! Scientists have imagined that a solar power station could be constructed in space, using miles and miles of solar cells. When light strikes a solar cell, it starts an electrical current flowing. In the solar-power space station, the electricity would be converted to microwaves, and then sent to Earth. On Earth, the microwaves could be changed back into an electrical current and sent to you through ordinary power lines.

So until the sun burns out — in about 20 billion years — you'll have enough power around to at least toast a marshmallow!

FOR MORE INFORMATION . . .

Places to Write and Visit

Here are some places you can write or visit for more information about fun machines. When you write, include your full name and address and be specific about the information you would like to receive. Don't forget to enclose a stamped, self-addressed envelope for a reply.

Discovery Center of Science and Technology
321 S. Clinton Street
Syracuse, NY 13202

American Museum of Science and Energy
300 S. Tulane Avenue
Oak Ridge, TN 37030

The Omaha Children's Museum
511 S. 18th Street
Omaha, NE 68102

Ontario Science Center
770 Don Mills Rd.
Don Mills, Ontario
M3C 1TC

Further Reading about Fun Machines

Here are more books you can read about fun machines. Check your local library or bookstore to see if they have the books or can order them for you.

Let's Make a Movie. Belgrano (Scroll)
Machines and How They Work. Weiss (Harper Junior)
The Magic Moving Picture Book. Bliss (Dover)
Mr. Bell Invents the Telephone. Shippen (Random)
Super Machines. Freeman (Silver)
Telecommunications Revolution. Storrs (Watts)
T.V. and Video. Irvine (Watts)
Undersea Machines. Stephen (Watts)
What Happens When You Make a Telephone Call. Shay (Contemporary Books)

Hands-On Facts about Fun Machines

Did you know . . .

• people in many places used lamps and fires as primitive telecommunications systems? During America's Colonial period, for instance, Paul Revere was instructed to light one lantern if the British were attacking by land and two if they were attacking from the sea.

• transmitters can now be used to send messages across the world at the speed of light, which is 186,000 miles (299,274 km) per second?

• the largest four-faced clock in the world is located in Milwaukee, Wisconsin, in the United States? Located on the Allen-Bradley Company building, each of its faces is 40 feet (12 m) in diameter.

• when you see a movie, you are actually seeing 24 still pictures per second? The sequence of pictures is interrupted by a shutter that blocks them 24 times each second just after each picture appears on the screen.

• music sounds better to us than most other sounds because the sound vibrations in music are regular and even, whereas those in non-musical sounds are irregular?

• the first accurate wind-up clock was invented in 1761 by John Harrison?

• the most accurate clock in the world is atomic? It is housed in the U.S. Naval Research Laboratory in Washington, D.C., and would take 1,700,000 years to gain or lose a single second.

• kaleidoscopes aren't used only as toys? They are also used to create new patterns for fabric, wallpaper, and carpeting.

• if you hold a hand over one of your eyes, everything you see will look flatter and more two-dimensional? Your eyes need to see two pictures at once to register depth.

GLOSSARY

afterimage: an image that seems to linger in the eye after the object causing the image is no longer in view.

atom: the tiny particle of which all things are made. Every atom contains electrons, protons, and neutrons.

circuit: a complete sequence of wire or some other substance for conducting electricity.

cornea: the transparent outer layer of the eye that protects the pupil and the iris.

electromagnet: a piece of iron that becomes magnetized when an electric current passes through wire wrapped around it.

electron: a negative particle of electricity that is a part of an atom.

iris: the colored part of the eye around the pupil.

kinetoscope: a simple machine used to move still photographs to make them appear to be moving in rapid sequence.

neutron: a particle of an atom that is neutral (without any electrical charge).

pantograph: a drawing machine that can be used to produce a larger or smaller version of an image.

proton: a positive particle of electricity that is a part of an atom.

pupil: the tiny opening in the iris that allows light to enter the eye and be reflected on the retina.

radio frequency: the speed at which radio waves oscillate, or swing back and forth.

ratio: a relationship between two things based on size or amount.

retina: a lining on the inside of the eye, containing rods and cones that are sensitive to light and color.

semaphore flags: flags used by the U.S. Navy to communicate between ships.

solar energy: energy made from stored heat that originally comes from sunlight.

solar panel: a panel placed on the side of a building that is warmed by the sun. In turn, the panel heats pipes underneath it. The pipes are filled with a liquid that is also heated in the process. The liquid heats water and air for the building.

sound waves: a series of movements in molecules that create sound.

stereoscope: a machine that holds two slightly different versions of the same scene before the viewer's eyes. This creates the illusion that the combined image is three-dimensional.

translucent: permitting the passage of light.

INDEX